The Rainbow and

The Rain

by
Paul Wootten

First published by Beauford House Books, an imprint of Eskdale Publishing, 2024

Illustrations created by Antony Wootten using Imagine Art
Book formatted by Antony Wootten

Find out about Paul and Antony Wootten's books here:
www.antonywootten.co.uk

Paperback ISBN: 978-0-9935042-5-9

Hardback ISBN: 978-0-9935042-7-3

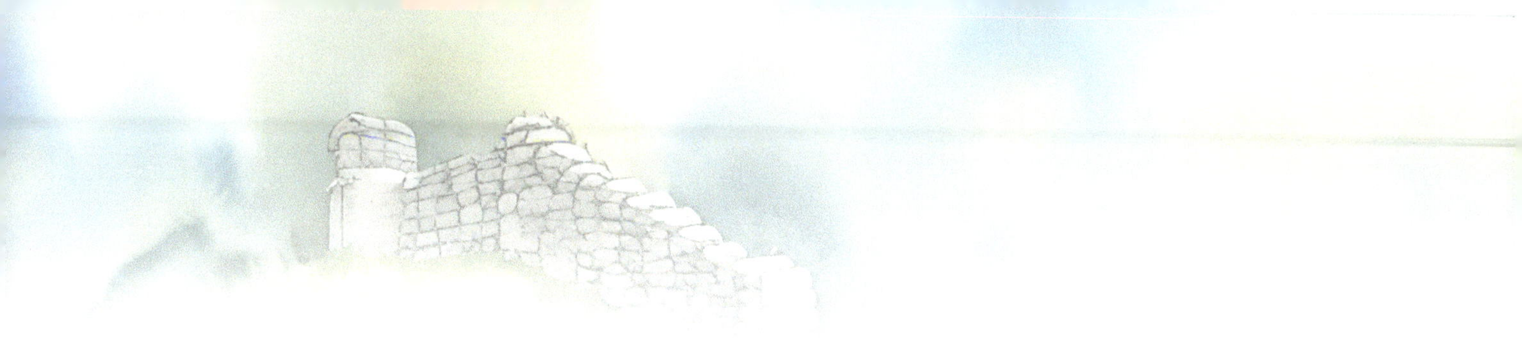

For Joan, my inspiration and support.

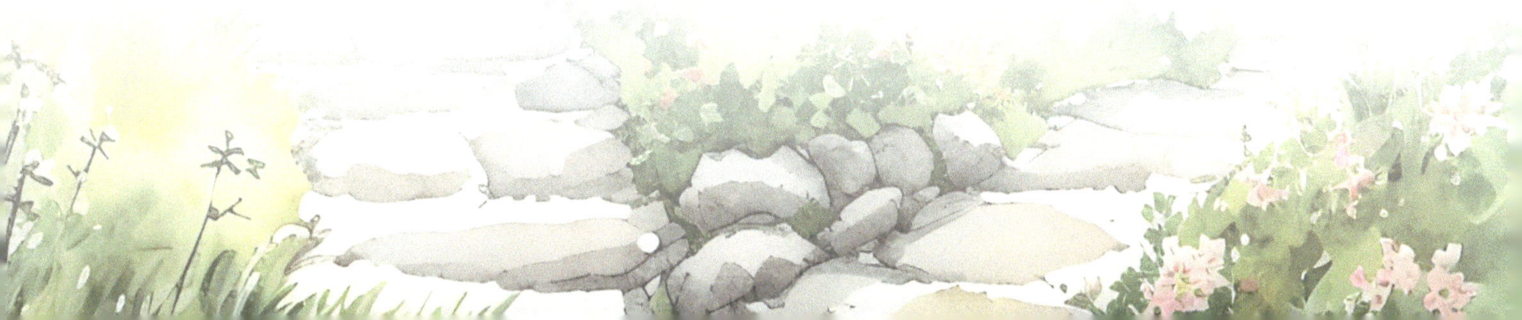

Contents

Sauce

I love to taste delicious words
Served up with onomatopoeia:
A sauce to slurp and gurgle through:
A banquet for the ear.

Forgotten

I visited The Tower yesterday,
And saw, etched clearly on its aging walls,
The things condemned men had to say;
An angry blast, a troubled sigh,
Merely a name and nothing more.
"Remember me!" each silence cried.
On cold, grey stone they worked their chore,
And then they died.

Outside the supermarket you can see,
Sprayed thickly on its concrete wall,
The things our young men have to say;
An obscene word, a gesture plain,
Just mindless smears that rise and flow.
"Remember us!" they scream again.
With aerosols they work in vain,
For we forgot them long ago.

Christmas Eve

This is the night of the year:
Night broken only by the rush of snow past the street lamps;
The whisper of its fingers as they caress the window pane.
Behind the glass a sombre silence lingers.
The Christmas tree and melancholy bank of holly wait in the darkness;
Berries like bloodstains nestle against deep-waxed, bottle-green leaves.
Baubles twitch in the window's draught
To catch a stray, mischievous chink of light from the slumbering fire,
And dance blues as deep as memory, green hollows of waiting,
Red festivals of expectation, and amber flames of desire.

Gilkicker

There is a hill beside the sea,
Washed gently on its lower reaches
By over-zealous spring-time tides.

Grassed to the shingle,
Where dogs and people mingle
With the prickly gorse and bramble
On a Sunday ramble.
Born of the war-clouds' rumble;
Hollowed out in concrete caverns
By the frightened and the feared.

Iron and steel inhabit
This home for rat and rabbit,
To wind and sea confined,
In Nature's web entwined,
To renew, each summer Sunday,
The city-blasted mind.

Gypsy

A tarmac patch behind some trees we call our home.
We don't stay long.
The people with the council papers always come.
And we move on.
My father mends the fences for the farms around.
We stay a while.
We spread all that we have about the ground.
You think us vile.
Our toilet is the hedge, our sink the running stream.
Our van is warm.
On winter nights we too can lie in bed and dream.

The Battle Of Pickering

On a gentle rise above the town the castle stands,

Its grey stone walls majestic in its solitude.

The casual visitor, amazed to find it, stares from the road,

And ventures in to taste the past.

Neatly grassed the outer ward invites

The picnic basket, and the tempted child to play,

(He climbs the motte ditch when the warden looks the other way.)

The keep smiles from the man-made hill,

Its walls which cannot stop a gaze

Are propped up for the view.

And there, below the bailey wall,

The well, that once refreshed the whole of Pickering

In time of need, lies quiet.

What ghosts haunt here?

The girl, whose trembling hand

Hauled on the rope as arrows flew;

The boy, who until now knew only how

To hold the oxen to the plough,

Whose fearful legs would not allow

Him to the wall again, hid here.

The whisper of their voices should be heard

Beneath the hawthorn, but no one stops.

They prattle past

And catch up with today around the shops.

The clash of metal biting metal;

The roar and tumult of the warring crowd;
The wild exchange of angry voices;
The scream of mighty engines straining loud;
The reek of hot exhausted air, make up the town.
The girl who cowers by the library wall as the world passes,
The boy who stops to share,
Just for a moment, the refuge offered there,
Are the spectres for tomorrow's visitors
Who will walk among *these* ruins unaware.

The Rainbow and The Rain

Run, you tiny drops of air
Fallen from grace and forced to share
with us this earthly place of rocks and mud.
Run down the mountain's aching sides to do us good
with new-born grass;
run with the shepherd to the dewy pond to pass
some time helping the sheep to live a little longer,
then on to the groaning town, growing stronger,
wrapping yourself round little boys to cool them down,
or gently bathe a lady's feet, or wash the fleas off dogs.
A fleeting time you have with us, no more.
Either you're off to wash some foreign shore,
or, your job done,
return to the air that gave you birth, caught by the sun.
Is this the way it is to be with us?
A ring of possibilities. No fuss.
We have our chance of pleasure and of pain.
We are the rainbow and we are the rain.

The Ragged Warrior

As he sits with his hands clasped under his chin and his blue eyes watching,
See not the ragged ends of his jeans, the thread pulled in his jumper, or his worn shoes.
Fix your eyes on the dark space inside the iris - look deep and see.
See the silver buckler hanging there with polished studs and leather straps;
See the gauntlets, steel wrought, wrapped round the lance; and on the shield
"I FIGHT INJUSTICE" boldly etched in gold.
And listen to his story, quietly told through pale lips,
Of finding homes for those who dwell in boxes,
Wintering beneath the motorway on concrete mattresses with overlay of Guardian or Times.
Money? "No!" he says, "There isn't any, but we do the best we can."
Yesterday he saved a wild addicted woman, today a lost inebriated man.
Yet here he sits in mild attire and tells me of the things he does,
No boast, just love of all mankind that drives him on.
Then off he'll go to mingle with the greedy crowds
Who do not know there is a warrior amongst them.

Hadrian's Wall

Stark, cold and permanent it climbs
From castle to tower, tower to castle, venting the Empire.
Like a lid on a fermenting pot it sits.
Close the gate and the Empire bursts,
But open to the waggon's rush,
To the breeze of traders on the open moor,
And peace of a kind remains.
It breathes the people in and blows them out.
But watch!
Watch where the bird hangs high over Crawfield Crag.
A shaft of light through the dark clouds gilds its wing
And holds him for a frozen moment out of time;
Locked like a tile in the great mosaic of the heather hills.
The cloud moves and the bird is gone.
Only the crag remains black against the gathering mists
With the great wall dipping and clinging to the cold rock.

Tomorrow

What will we do when the lights go out,
When all of the oil has been burned?
Will we sit in the darkness clouded with doubt,
When the last of our wheels has turned?
Will we look at the wind, the waves and the sun
And see the potential there,
Unlimited power for everyone
Now too busy to care?
Will we cry for the knowledge that just slipped away,
For the skills that our fathers knew?
It's all stored in computers that died yesterday
With the last breath the turbine drew.
And as the forests, already so small
writhe in smoke wreaths into the sky,
We shall to the caverns of yesterday crawl
And there we will probably die.
Oh wake up humanity! Where have you gone?
Begin now before it's too late.
Spend money, you misers, to capture the sun
Or we die like the coals in the grate.

They Blew the Bugle Early

The bugle blew too early:
I didn't have a chance
To hold you in my arms once more
To finish off the dance.
We had a fling at New Year
And danced our time away;
We caught the coloured ribbons
On that laughing day in May;
We galloped through the summer
When the foxtrot drove us mad,
But they blew the bugle early
That was all the time we had.

That bugle blew too early.
I didn't have the time
To love your Cinderella
In our final pantomime;
To sit with you and watch
The golden leaves dance in the air,
To take you in my arms again
And kiss your silver hair
As we glide across the ballroom floor
To the final dance of all,
Then quietly laugh together
As the darkening shadows fall.

But they blew the bugle early
And I couldn't wait to see
If you would give the honour
Of the last sweet waltz to me.

They blew that bugle early,
But you really mustn't care,
For when the Final bugle blows
I will be waiting there
To take you in my arms again:
There has to be a chance
To smooth away the years of pain
And finish off the dance.

Age

What will you do when you find I cannot hear

The gentle things you say: when I falter

In our conversation; cannot find the way

To frame my thoughts: when I stand

Holding out before me my uncertain hand,

Peering through failing eyes to view a world

I thought was mine? Or if I find,

Before ambition's cruel webs have turned to gossamer and drifted

Far beyond my caring, I should give way to weak despairing

Of what might have been. For never again

Will tomorrow bring "I can!" only "I did!" or, blacker still, "I should have done".

Will you smile and with a caring hand

Show, with your gentle words, you understand?

Or will you joy at my unbalanced gait?

"Here! Let me do it!" exasperated, in command.

Show it in everything you say and do,

And by my growing infirmity

Gain credibility for you?

Will it make you happy to point out

The things I cannot hear; whisper the words a little softer

As I struggle near; read out the words

You know I cannot see,

And stamp on my efforts with your victory?

Please see in me, my darling, when the winter comes,
The youth who ran to greet you from the train,
And held you close to keep the cold away;
Who laughed, with you, at all the others in the rain,
On holiday.

Together we must share these final years,
Declaring this statement of our bonded love.
Or nothing will have meaning, here or up above,
And we will wash away our past with all our tears.

It's Cold Outside

It's eleven o'clock and all is quiet.
The occasional car passes, hurrying home to supper.
Only the winter wind is busy in the street outside.
It nuzzles up against the house and moans in the chimney.
The bed is warm, and the bedroom light is as dim as dreams.
Somewhere a clock ticks in the house;
show-off! It would never dare to be so loud by day.
The radiator clicks, a floorboard groans,
a peace descends that only night time owns.
The night fizzes with frost that creases the puddles and cracks the tiles.
It forces the milk to push its creamy head out of the bottles,
bleary-eyed in its tilted night-cap.
Frost crisps the leaves and candies them with sparkles.
It thickens the twigs and spiders' webs with hairy coats of polar fur.
You can almost hear the cold singing, ringing with bell-like resonance
just beyond the range of human hearing.
But the bed is snug and the shadows in the room,
cast by the small lamp, are furry, warm and comforting,
made more so by the knowledge of the cold outside.

Fly

We settled in our pews in Sunday best and purpose firm,
Feigned interest in passages wrenched from some letters from St Paul.
All serious, we sat.
I watched with honest interest a fly soar up, quite unafraid, and circle round
the priest's head as he prayed for us.
No fuss for him as with the circling words his flight ascended.
I lost sight of him as the prayer, intended for our reclamation, ended.
Then, as we were asked to stand to sing, I saw him land.
His wing rainbowed the light an instant and
I rejoiced at the beauty of the thing.
Then up again he flew, nearer to God than I
That day, a solitary fly.

Teens

I see you now,
Holes in your jeans where your knees show through,
Watching the girls as they wander by.
You treat them with a kind of fear.
They do the trawling here today.
You wear your manhood in your ear
And simply hope they go away.
You've died your hair a shade of pink
And put a band around your neck.
In army boots, a size too big,
You watch them and have time to think
Of what you'd really like to be.
The television sowed the seed
Of flashy car and easy wealth.
To be a man that's what you need,
No point in working for yourself.

Oh, where is the little boy you were
With laughing face and eager eyes,
Willing to help with anything
No matter of its magnitude or prize?
You helped because to help was fun,
You wanted to be wanted then.

When did the others turn your head
To make you think the world of men
Was peopled with creatures spending
Half the day in bed?

Soon you will realise your mistake
When you have wriggled in their nets
And tasted a different kind of truth.
You'll find that your untutored brain too easily forgets
And jobs don't come to yobs in bovver boots.
So off to colleges you'll go
To learn the things that now you throw away,
Or work for a lifetime at some job you hate
To simply earn your pay.

Come, turn back the clock as quickly as you can
And learn from the boy you were
The way to be a man.

What Will Tomorrow Bring?

What will tomorrow bring out of its mystery?
What will tomorrow bring out of the dark?
Will it hold happiness golden as sunrise?
Will it bring joys that will soar like a lark?
Will it disperse all the tears born of sorrow,
Drying them up like the dew in the park?
Or will it with thunder-clouds darken my doorstep,
Cry with a sorrow despairing as rain,
Blast all my hopes with a gale of rejection,
Fray my desires in a blizzard of pain?
Today will soon lie in the pools of reflection,
But misty tomorrow is coming again.

Grail

Hanging beneath the towering crags:
A place of solitude,
Dark waters, still as ice and just as cold,
Reflect the granite walls that block the sun:
A lake, majestic in its mystery.
One vast tract of water nestling in the mountainside,
Flat as a full stop, clear as the sky,
Green as the earth, black as the hollow places that hide in crags.
The clearness of its depth rings in the mind and all is still,
Only the distant bleating of a sheep and the call of a bird
Disturb this hallowed quiet. This is a place of God;
A chalice filled with holy water,
Set before His great mountain altar,
Draped with cloth of clouds.
Standing here I am so small,
An insignificant dot beside a lake and a mountain wall.
And yet to be here is to understand;
To feel the truth;
To see the light for just one fleeting second.
I reach out my hand and it is gone.
But I was there.
The holy grail was lying at my feet.

Christmas

There is a peace on Christmas Eve
As if the world stands still,
When many a little girl or boy
Climbs up the wooden hill.
With weary eyes wide open,
And minds too full to sleep,
They tiptoe to the window,
Lift up the blind and peep
Out into the silent darkness,
Hoping there to see
Santa bringing presents
To fill the Christmas tree.

But in the softening darkness
The world alive with snow
Brings thoughts of another childhood
That began so long ago.
We have all heard the stories,
But standing here tonight,
With the snow so gently falling
Softly turning all things white,
They start to have a meaning
That was not clear before,
Of love for all the living,
The wealthy and the poor,

Of help for the weary traveller,
Warmth in a cattle shed,
While kneeling on a hillside,
Are shepherds filled with dread.
Wise men are on a journey.
We know what they will find.
When bringing Him their presents.

They slowly drop the blind.
Their minds turn to the presents
That Santa Claus will bring,
Then in the snowy cold outside
Some children start to sing.
With eyelids growing heavy
Just take another peep.
It's warm in bed,
"Goodnight, cold world
Of deep deep snow."
Deep sleep.

The Mark

The tinker left his mark out on the moor.
Whilst wandering in weekend pleasure,
Deep in green and sighing shade,
You would find it skulking in a hollow
A kettle or a carpet or the handle of a spade;
Worn-out things that no one wanted
Left to the weather and decay,
Left for the blanket grass to cover,
The bramble's arm to hide away.
Yes, they are signs that someone's been here,
Living where we want to walk,
Weaving dreams of forgotten people,
Threatening our silence with their talk.
                So
The councillor marked a piece of paper,
The surveyor marked a map,
The foreman marked time with his shovel,
The trees bled sap,
The grass groaned at the contemplation
Of its concrete overlay.
The council left its mark upon the moor
And there is no moor today.

MC

Talyllyn

The enthusiast he whistled
And the guard began to pray
As we started out for Tywyn
On the Talyllyn Railway.
The engine gave a mighty hiss,
The carriage gave a groan,
And we left the station master
On his platform all alone.
We were on the empty mountain side
Where the lonely buzzard calls
And the foaming water rushes madly
Over Dolgoch Falls.
Nant Gwernol and Abergynolwyn
Are in the mountains miles away
As Sir Handle bleeps his whistle
At the sight of Tywyn bay.
The sea we see from mountain walls
As our carriages complain.
With steam and railway memories
We all go back again.

Holiday

Frenzied, ice-cream ridden days of summer stretch away forever
On that first day I can call my own.
Lately risen, quietly caught beside the pool, stretched out in the sun
Noting the filter's drone. It has begun,
This time called 'holiday'.
The butterflies are busy round the yew,
Drawing attention to the berries that show its winter preparation.
On the road outside, the traffic moans a sonorous syncopation.
Yet here in the garden's peace the world stands still for me,
A lotus eater on a friendly shore
With just a swimming pool to represent the sea.
My dreams can rise to fill this seeping tide of pure monotony,
And I can be where most would long to be;
With ease unheard of, I can climb the peak,
Roll in the snow yet not become too cold,
Battle the bleakest winds and rise and fly
On the air-blast, yet still lie by the yew
With scant thought for the things I ought to do.
Yet as I dream, my own Odysseus comes, with whip in hand, once more
To drive me back to Attica's unhallowed shore.
The dream has gone; my holy day must dawn
And I must rise to go and mow the lawn.

Pain

In a shrieking ecstasy of pain,
Life springs into the world,
Hurled to show the pain of life in tears and crying;
Spends a lifetime wracked with bruises, cuts and sores,
Then leaves in one final act of pain by dying.

What god can give such pain to tear
The courage from a man, providing torture
For corrupt minds to plan the slowest death
With bamboo shoots and barbed wire?
The fire that warms us every day pulls tears of pain from blackened fingers,
While toothache lingers in its own mind-numbing way.

Life would go on so well if pain were gone.
Teeth could go bad, drop out
And we would barely know about it,
Save a little inconvenience. The senseless child
Could whittle his fingers to the bone for entertainment,
And appendicitis wouldn't matter 'till the last sacrament.

But pain is here and we were born to cry.
Without it we might make just one true happy smile
And then, still smiling, die.

Winter Nights

The rooftops changed their solemn greys and rusty reds for glistening whites,
This most wonderful of winter nights.
Lights leapt from yellow windows and danced in silence on the frosty paths.
Hearths poured out their comfort to huddled groups
Who laughed or slept away the winter's cold.
Bold spirits though, in clouds of vapoured breath,
Slid down the pavement's gleaming slopes
Or ran and laughed, fingers aglow, snowball making,
Shaking the icy whiteness from their hair,
Sharing their pleasures with the winter air.
But as the clock its later hours chime,
Peace returns: night's stillness muffled by the falling snow
That shows itself against the window's glow;
A white miracle of twinkling lights,
This most wonderful of winter nights.

Dew

Dew was on the land this morning,
Silvering the grass as the white mist
Hung in ribbons round the apple boughs.
The apples, ripe with reddened skins,
Hung heavily on drooping branches,
While tomatoes, still an envious green,
Watched from their canes.
Summer is here still with playful afternoons of blue and gold,
But the gold is slightly mellowed and the shadows lie much longer.
The leaves of the greengage have yellowed already.
Some garden birds we have already lost.
The dew was on the grass this morning,
Tomorrow the frost.

A Brief Memory of Ice

Through the misted glass I watched the rain.
It fell in slanting lines and danced in the wind,
Blurring the distance to a grey haze.
It caught in the hedge and dripped uneven drops upon the grass,
And caused the summer road to gleam again.

Time

You cannot see it go - imperceptibly it crawls,

Wrinkles the skin more than the sun,

Gnaws at the mind more than the bones; craving an answer.

And when it's gone there is no second go;

No 'try again - more effort needed'.

You either failed or made a good attempt.

None have succeeded.

All are brought to this eternal end.

What friendships you have made live on in the ether.

All else will crumble with the stones and turn to sand,

Then fall through the hour-glass measuring themselves.

Oceans dry, deserts fill with fruit.

Ozymandias returns a thousand times to do again what he did first.

Yet what you know, when all is said and done,

You rarely watch it go. You only know it's gone.

Autumn Cannibalism

We're eating last year's apples, picked this morning from the tree.
My family and I with ropes and buckets, cup-shaped upturned hands,
Happily descended on the orchard. Vast wealth of juice and pip and skin
Rose red, we gathered in our barrows.
The windfalls we left upon the compost heap,
With last month's marrows, to weep and rot.
But as I spread its peaty substance on the land in spring
Where all those apples are is never clear.
Yet I'm sure we'll pick them all again next year.

Christmas Warmth

Christmas came between two falls of snow.
One didn't linger long,
The other didn't seem to want to go.
And in the street outside it lies encrusted,
Heaped up along the gutter and right across the town.
It thrust itself, squeezing through the hedge
In massive folds, blown by the wind to drift and sigh
Against the window. The world goes silently to sleep
Each night beneath this blanket of softness.
The traveller floats by, unheard. Birdsong is muted.
The solitary barking dog thrusts back perspective
Through the searing cold. The old wrap thicker clothes
Around themselves and endure as they have always done before.
Behind their double window pane the young complain
In higher temperatures and summer wear.
Yet Christmas thrusts its own warmth everywhere.

Dream-time

From wherever to wherever, time is yours.

Spinning like threads of candy-floss,

Crossing and re-crossing loops of consciousness, opening doors

To where you were and where you want to be.

See where the light catches, flashing

Like silver scales, dashing down waterfalls.

Choose your light, and live again within the halls of yesterday. Nothing is what it seems.

From wherever to wherever, time is yours in your dreams.

Other World

Encaged behind giant marble-white pillars
I occupy hours exploring the walls.
My consciousness digs at the granite-grey fillers
That stop up the caverns and block up the halls.
I swim through the warm pools of bubbling foam,
That lie beneath warm cliffs, slimy and steep,
Then curl up and feel completely at home,
As the warm waves of darkness lull me to sleep.
But even in dreams you will find me a-wandering.
I explore every part north, east, west and south.
No minute will I ever be squandering,
Living inside the world of my mouth.

Melchior

Melchior - man of the metal mind -
Broods by the pulsar,
Hangs in infinity, a space crab with claws agape
Grabbing emptiness, watching with antennae eyes
The lights from stars, and calculating the beginning
Of things in playful recreation.
Set, he was, by a race of jellied beasts who blinked and died
And left no trace, save the metal man holding his location,
Counting stars. Occasionally he wonders why he hovers here.
He sighs to the darkness, calling to the gods who made him.
Here on this solid Earth, our telescopes embedded in the ground,
We hear his prayer and wonder why that pulsar makes a sound.

The Metal Man

He stands on the window sill, metal and plastic,
Little battery power packs and tendons of elastic,
Watching all my other toys playing on the floor,
Waiting for the moment when I walk through the door.
He knows that I will turn the switch that makes him twist and spin,
He knows that I will lift, with care, my special man of tin.
I will place him on the carpet and watch his eyes go round.
He will walk into my other toys and knock them to the ground.
Then when Mum says its time for bed, he'll go back on the sill.
I will lift the silver lever, and he'll stand up straight and still.
Then when I'm tucked up in my bed and Mum's turned out the light,
I will know my metal man is there, so everything's all right.

Hush Please

What a glorious day it has been today.
The trees in the garden are covered by
Bursting buds, and you should have seen the sky.
Blue, it was, as a sailor's eye.
"Hush, please!"

Do you remember the fun we had
Down in the forest when we were young,
You and I, and all those songs we'd sing,
And all through the thunder together we'd cling?
"Hush, please!"

Those winter nights when our friends came round.
The fire, roaring and hissing, was burning well
In the hearth, and the tales we used to tell,
And the jokes would make the laughter swell.
"Hush, please!"

Now isolate yourself away.
You sit with that glazed look low on your brow.
We've been here before you know,
Brain numbed by television's bright, dumb show.
"Hush, please!
Hush, please!!"

Memory's Morning

I watched This Morning, caught upon a wisp of air,
Carefree flung here and there, a filament of daydream's daughter's hair.
It lingered but a moment, transfixed in light, sight-locked,
Fingered only by memory's caress. Yet less for loss of moment,
Dulled and pulled from the mind's store, cold.

I hear, This Afternoon, gliding gently on a current slow,
Tasting the rushy hollows hiding places, loath to go,
Experience's afterglow, sliding and dipping round about,
Love loaded shouts of now.
How can they pass, dulled, lulled into yesterday's pain?
Only when memory's morning comes again.

Ghosts

Hear the snap of the latch, and the squeak of a board
With the sigh of the wind by the wall,
The crackle of sparks, as with one accord
They leap to the master's call.
The rocking chair creaks in the warming glow
As the kettle sings on the grate.
The wind in the chimney whispers low
And footsteps sound by the gate.
There's a turn of a key, and a step in the hall,
A breath of the autumn air.
The laughter of greeting, the welcoming call
of the plates full of comfort there.
The wind takes a turn, in the chimney it cries,
With time it has taken its share.
The house stands alone, open wide to the skies,
Making sounds from the elements, telling us lies.
For it's empty. There's nobody there.

Injustice

Sweated from the dark earth, cold and dry,
Torn by broken nails and blackened fingers.
Upturned, dirty faces seek the sky as the coal falls.
A cloud of midnight suffocation lingers,
Coating houses, grass and trees.
A smudge of daylight lifts and drifts carelessly, but no one sees,
Steeped in the poverty of darkness with just enough to eat,
A rotting roof, an old tin bath and aching feet.

It dripped from the roaring furnace, hot and bright,
Pulled with giant jaws in long extrusions.
Sweating faces marvel at the sight
As works directors draw their own conclusions,

Laying the profit on the ledger sheet.
The owner lies becalmed, beside the pool, in his retreat.
A smudge of dust drifts by to dim the sky.
Why should he care? The sun is in his eyes.

A New Pen

There is something rather special about a new pen.
I think it's very odd, but rather nice, to watch
The fine ink strands map out new worlds
And other lands from the imagination's eye,
Or cry the tears that lovers cry,
Or sigh for some forgotten thing.
A pen can bring a message from a foreign place,
"Wish you were here", or chase the random thoughts
That fill an idle mind, some kind, some cruel.
A tool of greater weight than any monster mover of our modern state.
It starts wars, and with its signatory flourish, wars can end.
A pen is champion of a cause, a bitter foe, or just a friend.

Progress?

Our lives are lived for entertainment.
Shallow realities haunt our dreams;
Interrupt our soaring fantasies.
Nothing now is really what it seems.
But wait! Gone is the gentle dream,
Woven by the dappled, woodland shadow,
Or glittered out on some deserted stream.
Our minds now need some powerful inducement,
Catching us all with radio beams,
Intoxicating us with instant pleasure.
Out from the television station teems
The deluge of pictures, all unthought, unfelt,
Yet vivid as our daily life, grim as despair,
Addictive as heroine, to kill the imagination.
Leaving our children's minds as empty as air,
Blank screens to show the shadows on.

The Monster

Deep in the night's desolate forest, a plaintive howl
Strikes terror in the ignorant heart.
Doors close, locks turn. Light up the fire
And let our hatred burn brighter than the eyes
That put fear into the darkness.
Light our brands. Call out the men,
And with their murderous hands destroy
The quivering prey. Dance away your strange rite
To the darkest gods. Become the wolf.
Stalk your easy prey. Then talk to take the guilt away.

There is a monster on the hill who hides
Away by night, then rises up to kill.
It stalks the field and meadow places,
Treads the river and the stream,
Sets each anxious heart aquiver.
It's a nightmare, not a dream.
It is tall and it is ugly,
Dealing death with either hand.
It spends its lifetime killing
Things it really does not understand.
As we hide in ditch and hollow,
It must have its daily blood.
Will its fangs reach down upon us,
As we're hiding in the wood?

Tell your children, and grandchildren
They must shun it if they can.
This menace to our green earth,
This monster they call man.

The Breaking

There was a howl of wind in the chimney and a flame leapt from the dying fire
as if in answer to its call. Peter placed another log to catch its flicker,
bringing some heat back to the room. The winter's cold was creeping in again
and he had been dreaming of times long past. He had not noticed the fire.
"That's the last one, son," his mother's voice came softly from the shadows.
The gnawing flames on the new log showed her face smiling at him,
her silver hair reddened by the warm glow.
"OK Mum, I'll go and get some more."
"Wrap up warm, mind," and she smiled again.
The snow was falling in squally blasts, and was already knee deep
where the fence had stopped its flight.
He pulled his coat more tightly round himself,
screwing his eyes against the biting wind. At least he could see.
The snow had lit the dark hollows with its brightness,
and the log pile, slowly being covered, stood out clearly.
Log fires and candlelight, and the year 2000 had long passed.
It need not have been like this, he knew. Recollections of his dreams
from earlier that evening came flooding back to him.
They didn't have to do it. But his father had been there and he had agreed
so probably it was for the best. But look at what they had.
Light at the flick of a switch, moving pictures that talked to you
from a magic box. They even say that people then could fly.
He found that harder to believe. Oh yes, he had seen the pictures
of those funny, silvery things, like great fish with wings.
But they must have been too heavy, far, to fly.

What was it his father used to say? Something about having gone too far,
knowing too much. It was then they had decided upon the breaking.
Everybody did it. All over the world. First it was the weapons.
Terrible things they must have been.
Mother says they could have destroyed the world many times over.
Well, when they had all gone the people realised
that the knowledge to make them still remained.
They decided to step backwards and destroy the power forever.
The power. Oh, what a wonder it must have been
flowing through those humming wires to heat the houses,
cook the meals and make the magic boxes work.
People could talk to each other across miles and miles with the power.
Still, it's gone now, and everything else with it. Another gust of wind
caught him in the face making his eyes sting.
His icy fingers clutched at the damp logs. He filled the basket
then stumbled back to the house. The sweet smell of fresh bread
was carried on the warm air that melted the snow in his hair.
He threw two logs into the heart of the fire. They hissed and spat as the snow leapt from the heat.
The kettle, singing quietly on the hearth, changed its tune
and sang a song of fresh brewed tea.
"Is everything all right, son?"
"It's ok, Mum", he said as he rejoined her by the fire.
He watched the flames leap, felt the warmth around him, and listened to the storm outside.
"Isn't it great to be alive, Mum?"
"Oh yes, my son, it certainly is."

The Lock

A mist was on the water,
And though the river still was sharp and clear,
The rivulets and reaches disappear
As we pass round the point to face the lock.
There, with a shock and scurry of water,
We see it as the racing stream catches us in its eager grasp
To plunge us on the rocks or gently lead us
Through the safety of the lock.

The ticking clock slows down.
Then we at once are with the others
Fighting on that flurried water;
All alone though we're with others
Guiding bows between the pillars.
Fear mounts as the black gates shudder.
Fevered excitement is riding high.

"Will she strike?

Will she strike?" I cry with strangled voice.

The moon drops below the trees and all is still.

The turmoil now is over.

The clock ticks at its normal pace.

There's no disgrace, and no one cried.

We will emerge on the other side

To drift on the cold and lifeless stream.

The mist has gone, but so's the dream.

Teaching Machines

(Just prior to the onset of computers in school the Teaching Machine was being paraded as the ultimate tool for mechanized learning. It set the scene for some of the teaching aids used today where facts are regurgitated as simplistic responses to banal questions: enquiry into the essence of an historical character can sometimes be lost. I saw this question, and just had to write this poem.)

Waterloo the fight: now name the man ...

 Mud and filth and broken wheels of battle
Spread across that ghostly, losing land.
There, where the shattered light of hope
Dipped like the sun into hungry sand,
Leaving men and children lying where
That fugitive from Elba fought his last,
And passed into discredit like the cold bones of his men,
Alone in dark fields under the stars.
Who were they who fought for him and lost,
Fostered from the youth of France to bleed or flee?
Were they like you and me, with dreams of life
far from the field of death?
And what of him, fanatic though he be,
To lead them through this vast adversity to this?
What bliss he knew? What thoughts could drive him on?
The machine would only say

…Napoleon

Time: No Time

The evening light retreats before the more persuasive arguments of blackness,
Leaving a plunging pit of turbulent questions unanswered
Pounding at the temples for time.
No time!
The dusky anaesthetic gently forces firm eyes to close, numbing sensations.
Fingertips become elbows when locked in a cushion land, feeling the velvet folds of darkness
Overcome the silk-white brilliance of the artificial moon still burning out of sight.
Deep in the pit of burning questions the changing figures move
Like locomotives in a tunnel. They start a spot of light
That grows crashing in the mouth to call "Who am I?"
To a silent world that cannot answer.
Still faster, patterns change, till left at last on a country lane,
Like a fish in a bowl of trees, facing the fountain rose blossom
Bursting beside the road with its temptation;
"Steal a rose: a rose: a rose"
A rose bursts into shadowy light,
Cascading answers on tired eyes that do not grasp their meaning.
Silk-thin reality has returned.
The velvet answers seep beyond grasping hands,
As this sober world expands into an illusion of things,
And I awake.

Self Haunting

Before me in the dark and hollow church he sat

Watching the sinking rays of sun that streamed through the window

To his seat in the clutching pew. Alone, he knew it too.

Separated by three empty rows from the concentrated congregation.

"Who's that, Mrs Jones?"

Mrs Jones is visiting the moon, She'll be back soon

To chant a prayer, or hear the banns, or make her weekly recitation.

"He's the prodigal, returned," a hesitation.

His face was not towards the pulpit strained,

But his thoughts and eyes were here together trained

On the floor of the gilded aisle.

I thought I saw a passing smile as he slightly turned his withered head.

Once, with a young bride he walked here on the darkening floor.

I turned my eyes towards the door

And saw them standing, her in white

With pale features echoing the coming night.

She smiled; and now he's all alone

With no one to mend the torn coat or soothe the swollen hands.

Tired of the cold stone beneath his back,

Lacking a home, he had fallen on this familiar track.

The service over, reluctantly I know,

I stayed behind to watch him ache to go.

He turned at last, when stars were fully blazing in the skies,

And I gazed vacantly into my own eyes.

Evening

The bustle of the day is done.

The dogs have seen off the fox from the yard.

We battled through our tasks and won or lost,

too much to do: too hard to count the cost.

But now the light has gone, the rhythm changed,

the pattern of our life is rearranged.

No bustle now, we sit and think, lie back in our chair, clutching a drink and listen to the whispers in the dark;

a simple spark of memory that blazes up momentarily to catch the senses,

thrill to a smell, shiver with the cold, lie in the sun, relive a story told by someone precious.

Let us linger on these memories awhile, smile at the antics of a child,

wonder at the wildlife to be found outside where the ground slips down to the trees.

Remember the snow that lay there freezing, disinclined to go;

the trees' fine tracery of black and white framing the rooftops and the moon.

The fire changes its tune as a log settles.

The dog shifts in sleep, his feet twitch as he chases the dream-fox out of the ditch.

I stretch, I close my eyes: then everywhere is peace.

Cornwall

The surf flies over cliff-tops as it thumps the shore.
Short wind-blasted trees lean over the road, sore
of leaves awaiting April's tenderness. But now
The rain beats down upon the hill, relentless in its driving
beneath lowering clouds that almost graze
it with its passing, here as the light fades.
The tower of a long forgotten church scrapes the sky
as the high downs curve. Sea in front
and rolling emptiness behind where the road slips by.
Nothing lives here where the cruel wind rules;
only the ghosts drift past, in wisps of whitened spume
kicked from the sea, or, voiceless, scream through rattling branches.
Only the greedy merchant or the fool treads here.
The empty road ends in the hollow places where the people are.
When summer comes and the hill-top bakes in unrelenting sun,
hundreds will come to climb the rocky tors and with the deer will run
the moors that now they shun.

Thyme Travel

Small green leaves as pale as a memory,
wafting a perfume completely sublime.
Caught by the wind, the leaves give a tremor.
We pick them and crush them, then travel through time.
Thrills of the past come crowding before us,
olfactory pictures as silent as mime.
Great Sunday dinners rush out of our childhood,
plates filled with chicken and parsley and thyme.

Memories flood from times of privation,
coal fires and ration books, windows of ice,
but fun in that one simple room that was heated
and smells from the kitchen would tempt and entice.
Faces of friends pass by in an instant.
Christmases, summers are gone in a trice.
All just a flash in a moment of memory
stirred by a flavour more precious than spice.

Forever One

When you want me I'll be there, watching from the mirror while you do your hair,
holding your uncertain arm upon the stair.
Don't look for me, just know that I will caress your window with the winter snow,
and be beside you everywhere you go.
With the scent of apple blossom in the spring, in the songs that children's voices sing,
and the smiling treasures that their faces bring,
I will be with you, if you're wanting me. Just look in the quiet parts of your memory,
and there, together, you will see us, still watching the rain fall on the windowsill or walking with
the dogs on Beacon Hill.
When time becomes unravelled by the sun, the love we've shared can never be undone
because we were, we'll be forever one.

Litter - A View From a Window

You dropped your litter on the ground, then looked at it and walked away,

leaving it to creep, windswept, towards the verge, where it would stay to join the heaps of other's carelessness.

You watched it go. You saw the speckled white remains dotting the grass, and just passed on your way. I had to stay to watch the papers sway amongst the grasses, catch in a bush, play a while then, finding the wind, crawl off to lie beside the wall.

I have to ask. Would it have been too hard a task to have picked it up, when you saw it fall?

If we cannot do these simple things, we have no hope at all.

The Cherry Tree

Tiny petals are falling from the cherry tree,
freed by the wind. They scatter down a brilliant white,
disguising the ground, bringing back memories of winter,
with slow falling snow-fall, painting the garden.
But this will not harden into ice.
Bathed in the sun; no fun of snowmen standing here
to cheer the spirits; no snowballs to play though the frigid air,
but warming our hearts a different way.
Nostalgia, from glorious remembered Christmas times,
is here, once more, to lift the day.

Charlie

Charlie is my little dog,
He's black and white and tan.
Never was a better dog since the world began.
He helps me in the garden when I'm digging up the weeds,
and he helps me in the greenhouse when I'm planting out the seeds.
He helps me in the summer house when I sit down for tea.
He has a little drop as well as he's always there with me.
He walks along beside me, and every now and then
will look up at me, reassured he carries on again.
I sit down of an evening to doze beside the fire
and Charlie sits and guards me, he never seems to tire.
He'll often sit upon me and slowly go to sleep.
He's warm and soft and wonderful. It makes me want to weep
to think that there will come a time when Charlie won't be there,
He won't be running past me as I climb up the stair,
He won't be waiting by the bed to guard me through the night
or wake me in the morning to show everything's alright.
But Charlie is my little dog
and every day is fun.
He'll stay with me forever,
My pretty little one.

The Toy Train

Fresh in pristine polished glory,
it gloats its way around the track,
crosses the tin-plate level-crossing
to make a cracked and battered tractor wait,
then on to the town.
The farmer with his dog watches from the gate where the cow grazes.
The miller stands beside the mill and gazes as the train passes.
Outside the White Horse they sit with raised glasses,
to celebrate the train, possibly, or to toast the bride
outside on the grass by the little church.
Lurching on, it climbs over the bridge and stops in the station
where the postman watches with his sack.
There's a faint clack as the signal changes.
The engine whirs in pristine polished glory
and gloats its way around the track,
crosses the tin-plate level-crossing
to make a cracked and battered tractor wait,
then on to the town.

Part Of Me's a Gypsy

Part of me's a gypsy and I love the open air,
the chance to wander freely in the woods without a care,
a chance to stand for hours on a hill and simply stare
at all the glories that surround us, free for all to share.

Part of me's a gypsy and I love a fire so bright
when it's burning in the garden on a very frosty night,
and the moon is casting shadows with its rather ghostly light,
but the dark above is pricked with stars, Orion's belt's so bright.

Part of me's a gypsy and I love the open road,
a chance to visit places that the travel brochure showed,
the pace of life, so hectic, by my gentle travel slowed,
through caverns rich with memories where ancient waters flowed.

Part of me's a gypsy -
Gosh! What have I just said? -
I'd rather sit beside my fire, in my land-locked home, with my soft, warm bed,
and let the television feed my mind with pictures here instead.

Whitby

The wind from the sea scours the land.
Gulls sweep the air and hang fast against the surge.
Their urgent cries fill the hills with vampire dread.
In blackened cloaks and silver chains the undead walk through the town,
pause to buy chips at The Magpie,
then off to the beach to catch the blow.
Slow monsters of the deep glide on the tide,
Wide-stacked with vast containers filled to feed a hungry world.
Curled up in their caravans the sane remain,
sealed in tin contentment from the driving rain.

Sherwood

Deep in the forest shade,
where the shadows blacken the view,
you can hear the trees talk.
Listen to the trees.
At first they whisper as the breeze passes,
and, while the whispers fill your ears,
the trees engage your mind.

This space that now contains yourself
held deer and boar and forest elf.
Knights on horses blundered through
this clearing occupied by you.
Outlaws laughed and maidens cried,
arrows sang and soldiers died.

This brown earth, hard beneath your feet,
supported lovers here to meet
in safety from the sheriff's gaze.
Robin's horse would quietly graze
beside the track where now you stand.
Marion would take his hand and
here together they would make their vows.

Is it magic that allows you to share
this moment with the moving air?
Or do we leave our image everywhere,
and the trees, spreading their roots deeply through the ground,
soundlessly read the stories of the past
to tell, at last, in whispers to the eager wind?

Where Are the Streets?

Where are the streets that I walked in my youth,
with their quiet country gardens, and tea on the lawn?
They have all disappeared in a cloud of exhaust,
and lines of parked cars are all you can see.
No more Christmas trees behind bay windows.
Christmas now spills out into the street
and people drive by and say how sweet it is to see
the pretty reindeer and the stuffed child on Santa's knee;
see the garish blue electric icicles flickering on the guttering:
stuttering neon nuisances that cheapen the story.
Where is the glory of the poor boy in the stable
and the children able to gaze at the vivid stars in the velvet black
now lost in street-light grey? Back gardens never see the night:
fierce fluorescent light predicts our tread
and conquers even midnight with synthetic day,
lest we should encounter something dreadful in the dark.

When summer comes we either stay indoors
or seek the sun on foreign shores.
The roads are full of monsters breathing death:
breath-catching beasts that line the kerb and stop the games.
How glorious it was for us to play kerbo and tag across the road,
sure that our playground there was safe, no car showed up from one day to the next.
The only obstacle that vexed our mums was dropped by horses.
The garden gates stood open to the world and we hurled about in camaraderie.
Everyone knew everyone and we were free to leap and run.
Today, locked in fear's protective bubble, no one ventures out,
The street no longer is a place to play. Only the layabout will shout,
disturbing the peace, as we huddle behind the curtains, out of his way.
The gardens now are all of manageable size. No time for tea out there,
no time to mow a lawn. Concrete slabs and decking fill the space.
No place here to lark about: you must go to the park.

It isn't very far, but even so, we take the car.

Good Morning!

I always say, "Good morning," to everyone I meet
when walking down a country path or out along the street.
My mother who told me sternly all the things I ought to know
said, "It's dogs who skulk in corners; people say 'hello'"
My mother said I had to and my father showed the way
to greet a fellow citizen. He'd often say, "Good day."
He'd sometimes say, "How are you?" or something of the kind.
To just walk past in silence, would not have crossed his mind.
The people he was greeting would treat him just the same.
Quite often they would raise their hats or call him by his name.
Now I've grown up I feel it only right to do that too.
To keep up the tradition, it's the friendly thing to do.
But the people I am meeting just silently walk past,
pretend they haven't heard me and pass by rather fast.
People with their children will hurry them away, with, "oh"
or "eh?" the only things that they can find to say.
Yet if the people you are passing have a dog or two,
They will often be the first to speak a greeting aimed at you.
They will surely say, "Good morning. What a lovely day."
They'll even stop and chat awhile before they move away.
So somewhere in the future, as the generations go,
it will be the kids who skulk in corners
and the dogs who say, "Hello!"

The Deer

He looked at me, dark eyes, intelligent, questioning.
Just for a moment of time two creatures of
alien species paused to recognise each other's existence.
His head held high, muscles rippled beneath brown fur
catching the morning light as he stood in the road.
I sat locked in metal meditation, gazing through glass,
the engine humming in neutral stillness.
In that instant his stare was, not at bonnet or bumper,
but laser-sharp into my eyes.
Young and confident, enjoying the glory of its own skill and beauty,
It took one bound, cleared the hedge
and disappeared amongst the dappled trees.
I, glorying in the wonders around me,
continued my journey.

The Flag

My flag is of Great Britain
The red, the white and blue.
I fly it with great pride you know,
As other people do:
When wars are won, on jubilees and when we win the cup,
On any time when I believe the country's looking up.
A flag is just a symbol of the love and truth and care
And honour for each other that some people try to share.
My flag is on a flagpole, some people have a badge,
For some it is a football shirt, for others, camouflage.
Children need a flag to fly to help them feel secure,
But the flags that they are flying now aren't like the ones before.
The labels on the clothing show to which camp they belong,
And woe betide the lonely lad who goes and gets it wrong.
For some it is a haircut, for others it's a pin,
And who they are is obvious from what it's sticking in.
For some it is the way they speak, for others what they drink,
But rarely has it much to do with anything they think.
In Ireland they threw bottles at the soldiers in the street,
Because their grandads threw them it made them feel complete.
But any sign of honour or love or simply care
Is lost among the adverts of what they want to wear.
Now the flag is more important than what it's standing for:
Instead of ending conflict it's the thing that starts the war.

70

Mole

So tiny;
black as midnight,
scurrying between the nettle clumps,
nose to the ground.
No sound
as the velvet coat
strokes the leaves and dry grass,
you pass unnoticed by the world.
Curled in your bed
you spent the brightness of the day.
But now,
as evening dulls the sun
and sends the shadows,
you leave your hole.
Mole.

The Wind

What has touched this bitter wind searing through the dappled grasses,
Roaring across the open fields,
Catching the scent of coffee as it passes;
Fussing about the field's edge, dredging up litter?

Did it rise where the polar bear rides the melting pack ice,
Chasing seals to feed her cubs,
Catching the gnashing, clawing power with a slice
Through the settling snow to blast it skywards?

Did it cross the sea and surge around the little boats,
Bouncing and twisting them from their purpose,
Catching the curses from the sailor's throats,
Picking the salt from the wave tops and hitting the cliffs?

Then did it rise to the tops of the mountains, heather-scented rainbow-painting wonder,
To wander with the shepherds and catch the smell of his sheep?

Or does it rage through the steep gorges hunting us,
To fill our world with its mischief and its memories?

To The Beach

"To the beach", the white arm on the wooden sign read.
Those three simple words conjured their magic,
and off we ran with pulses racing,
out-pacing each other to be first to spy
the gleaming emptiness, the sky-reflecting wonder
of sighing ripples and wave-stroked sand.
But if the tide was in we'd have to stand and listen
to the whoosh of the waves and the suck of the shingle.
On the promenade our voices mingled with the funfair fanfare,
and in the air, candyfloss and diesel, salty rocks and ice-cream.
The scream of gulls and children's voices,
the whip and crack of a kite biting the air sang around us
as we watched the receding tide.
Then, buckets in hand, our naked feet
tenderly trod the pebble paining perfection
to reach the wet sand and sink in the soothing softness there,
with thoughts of sand castles, cold skin, wet trunks, ice cream,
and sandy towels to scour our modesty.
Eventually in gritty-shod satisfaction
we took the path marked "To the car park".

73

Winter Sun

A watery winter sun wakes the world with the wonder
of golden-speckled spiders'-webs and silver dew.
Few will see the sparkle and the drips of light that let the leaf dance.
Yet there is a chance, if you wake early and step out on the damp grass
to pass beneath the dripping trees, and taste the perfume on the air,
that you can share this moment with the singing birds.

Wind, Rain and Sun

Wind - flutters, booms, whistles, whines,
blunders, whispers, growls,
grumbles, rumbles, slaps, thunders,
twitches, tumbles, howls.

Rain - tickles, tinkles, taps, patters,
smacks, dribbles, plops,
trickles, rattles, spits, spots, splutters,
pings, pops, splashes, flops.

Sun - warms, flashes, blazes, melts,
burns, peeps, streams,
stares, gilds, glimmers,
heats, browns, beams.

Gen's Song

(As an old man, Gen remembers his childhood when he walked the land with Jesus.)

Now he has gone the grass is not as green, the trees are not as tall,
the mountains rise, the rivers fall.

Now the wind that blows, blows empty through the hall.

We ran together through the meadow grass, and climbed the trees.
We battled with the rain on windy seas,

Now the wind that blows, blows empty through the trees.

But, He was here, He touched my hand,
His feet strode out across this land,
He blessed the trees, the mountains and the streams,
and sowed the seed of glory in my dreams.

First

Guided by the sun, while it streaks across the starry sky
flying to near oblivion through the searing air,
just a point of light that makes the people stare.
Touch it. You can be the first to hold this fragment of forever, once it's cold.
Each fold on the blackened stone etched by the air,
holds memories of how we all began.
Run your fingers on the pitted blackness there
and see the sparkle in the crystal specks that no one else has seen.
In flight the blinding light had hidden these things from view.
The only one to see them yet is you.

Hold the craggy oyster in your hand,
mud-coloured monster stranded on the sand.
Prize with your knife and in the fleshy paleness, see
the glory of the small white pearl in infant purity.
No hand has touched, no eye has seen the light
play on its silky surface or seen its pinky sheen.
The thrill of exploration bursts upon you. You are the first.

The little brown pip that slipped through my fingers
when I cut the apple lingers long enough for me to admire its shiny beauty.
It had nested snug in its satin bed for six long months.
No eye had seen it grow, no hand had touched till it touched mine.
This symbol of perpetual life that could eventually become a tree
was seen by no one else but me.

Memories In a Stable

Icy wind is filled with dancing specks of brilliance,
some rising, some falling steadily, sharp and biting,
bringing stinging pain to the bare patches of skin
revealed when the wind catches the thin cloth and whips it away.
Some respite when a wall shields the road,
or a house-side looms large to stop the blast.
But that is fast away and the open heath
condemns them to the elements again.
The night is lit with snow. Even the low shadow-places
that have shunned the sun stand stark before this white relentless light
that points the way, not to a castle with its stout grey walls and roaring fires,
not even to the nestled comfort of a cottage beneath thick insulating thatch,
but to the bare scratched walls of a stable carved from the earth.
Its clay and rocky walls at least will keep the wind away.
There is warmth here, not the warmth of fire and smoke,
but the honest warmth of fur and flesh and steaming breath.
There is comfort here, not the comfort of other folk, soft beds,
and flea-flecked blankets in a grubby room,
but the clean comfort of fresh straw, deep and soft, filling the air with its own perfume.
The first taste of this world for the just-born
is the grain-stemmed dust that could be formed
into bread or steeped into browning ale.
The first smell is of warm, pale skin and the honest breath of cattle.
Not for Him the smoke-filled debauchery of the mean little houses
packed with sweating humanity, stacked with greed and fear.

The first sound He will hear is the rustle of the straw,
coupled with the hollow stomp of cattle feet,
and the deep snort of animals greeting His arrival with a cloud of steam.
Or can He hear other sounds: the stars singing
in the icy sky above or the angels in the very air around?
And His dreams, what could His dreams be?
Would they be filled with the soft feel of His mother's skin
and the fresh taste of her sweet, warm milk?
Or could they be filled with eternal memories of what has been and what is still to come?

The Air Is Cold

The air is cold, the air is still.
The singing stars the heavens fill
Against the blackness of the night.
Through clouds of breath we view the sight,
The air so cold each movement rings,
Making glockenspiels from common things.
Toes and fingers lost to ice,
Like razorblades the cold will slice
Through cotton, fleece and supple leather,
Out in the garden in this weather.

A Miniature in Time

(The Chateau de Chantille is a magnificent French chateau filled with works of art. One miniature in a case of miniatures peered up at me.)

I saw you watching me through the glass.
I felt your pain. No plain clothes for you;
high fashion draped in silken splendour
swept in gorgeous folds to hide your tiny feet;
high hair, styled by the best in France, sets off your face;
lace cuddled your chin, and rouge concealed the pallor
of your haughty cheeks. But in your eyes was fear.
This cameo lends immortality. As you sat watching the artist
dip his brush, with each minute stroke he captured you in time,
He could not conceal the anguish of your aristocratic line.
Behind your eyes, glinting in the oil's soft sheen
I see the shadow of the guillotine.

Abbotsbury

(Margaret's Retreat)

Upon a hill beside the sea the chapel stands,

tall-roofed against the driving wind,

a beacon for the little ships that seek a safe way home.

Down at the water's edge the tiny people,

ant-like, mingle with the shadows from the passing clouds.

Loud-crying gulls soar high around the hill,

while white doves coo on the sun-warmed grey-stone windowsill.

Beneath the hill the village lies,

tucked in a crease of rolling green that shields it from the weather's rage

and the thunderous roar of the driving sea.

Thatch snuggles down on stone, and wraps itself round window frames.

The little school, now filled with ghosts,

still serves, with tea and cakes, the curious,

whose minds are filled with memories of children's voices raised in praise,

or scuffing playground feet of those engaged in laughter, shouts and games.

Their names are gone, their pegs are empty now:
only their spirits soar to haunt the tarmac, brick and bright blue toilet doors.
Narrow pavements separate the pretty gardens from the busy road,
and tiny lanes run up into the hills.
Sweet smelling rosemary spills over red-brick walls.
White gravestones line the church from end to end,
and from the rugged tower, braced with crenellations,
a jackdaw calls the faithful to attend.
Like toys in a miniature town the people gather,
there is no need to hurry, children pull and chatter,
nothing seems to matter, here in Abbotsbury.

Senlis

(Senlis is a small well preserved medieval city with Roman origins in Picardie Northern France. Much restoration work has been done to keep the medieval flavour of the place. The Saint-Pierre church is undergoing restoration, and the masons have cleaned much of the stone work, but even they could not completely remove the bullet holes along one side of the tower wall.)

The mason's craft, though sweet and true,
Cannot completely clear the view
of bullet desecration, deeply bored
like woodworm on an old oak door.
Its smooth and yellow stone alone
bears witness to its fearful past.
Each stone forever wears upon its face
the damage of the blast.
This place was conflict-formed,
with two concentric walls of stone
protecting those lone Romans from the wrath of Gaul.
All through the wicked years
of inquisition, its position held,
felled only by the Nazi's vile oppression.
No grinding hand can sand away the sight;
no prayer, rising from the chapel floor, can put it right.
Ghosts of the past still walk the narrow streets
and sigh with the breeze across the cobbles full of memories
in the dream time of the night.

Bury Me Beneath The Trees

Bury me beneath the trees,

so through their mottled leaves,

the breeze will sing me to my sleep.

Do not weep. Know that, down amongst the roots,

I shall be part of the world and all its secrets share.

There, where the Romans fought and mailed knights walked,

I shall touch each time, and taste the past with all its mystery

to make it mine.

Christmas Decorations

Today I have to take the decorations down.
The lights on the tree that shone out into the dark streets
go back in the box for another year.
The streamers that hung across the room reflecting the light
will not be there tonight.
Each bauble tells a story.
Glorious reflected sparks of memory
cast us back to taste and smell and feel the colours:
The little yellow bells that move in the rising air
catching your breath as if a ghostly hand is passing there;
The pretty cottage with its door and single window pane
slip you back again to the carol-tinctured air
of the country store where you found it.
"Can we have it, Mum?" And she is there again, though long gone now,
to hold your hand, and did she understand
that it would lend her immortality?

The deep blue ball of fragile glass
that now has lasted sixty years,
gently wrapped and placed beside the paper cracker
that still rattles out the mystery of what's inside.
Each precious treasure now is put aside,
each memory addressed,
each tiny item, vast as empires, lovingly caressed.
The box is closed, its light not dimmed but out of sight.
Its hidden glory we must just remember,
until it bursts upon the world again next cold and dark December.

Where Are You Going?

Where are you going out there in the roadway?
Where are you going out there in the dark?

Are you taking a lorry up onto the motorway,
on to Southampton, where you will embark
on a boat bound for countries across the wide channel
to Holland or France or a long run to Spain,
to fill up with flowers or cheeses or lemons,
crates of fine claret, then come back again?

              Or
Is it a bus full of people you're driving,
some rich and some elderly home from abroad,
where they spent all their money soon after arriving,
at the parks and museums they simply adored?
Now they go home to their sweet little houses,
where day after day they will moan and complain,
till as the year turns in the humdrum and boring,
they can get on your bus and go travelling again.

                    Or
Have you just been to a twenty-first birthday,
out in the countryside, not very far,
where all of your friends just begged you to stay,
but you had to leave quickly as you had your dad's car,
and you wish that they hadn't forced all that beer on you,
weren't they aware of the dangers of drink?
Now in the dark you are careering homeward,
where you'll rush to the kitchen to be sick in the sink.

These are the thoughts in the dark that consume me
when I hear all the traffic go past out of sight:
where have they come from and where are they going;
and does it still matter? Not really. Good night.

Behind The Fire

Behind the fire, where the chimney curves black with soot, the pictures form.

Tiny at first, just crimson stars that flare and fade,

Then, castles cling to fiery crags,

Or broomsticks fly with ugly hags,

Tearing the blackened night to rags.

Rockets take off into space

Through galaxies of orange lace,

Changing to a simple face.

A letter forms and then another,

Mother, father, sister, brother,

All paraded in the night,

With this panoply of light.

When all is done, the fire slips down to clinking embers glowing red and gold.

No one remembers the stories that it told,

Just happy on this winter's night, content and warm.

Old Man

Remember me, not as I am now,
With stooping back and furrowed brow,
With hair as grey as polished steel,
With all the aches and pains I feel:
Myopic stare and shuffling gate.
No longer can I imitate
The young who laugh and shout and play.
But I could once. I had my day.
I could run and climb and swing.
I thought I could do anything.
I could ride a bike all day
And still have energy to play
Or sing around the fire
As the flames grew higher and higher:
Toasting apples in the dark
And climbing mountains for a lark.
Running barefoot by the sea,
The seventh wave would not catch me.
But who did catch me? Father Time.
He crept up like a nursery rhyme
And stole my strength, wrinkled my skin.
In the end we all give in.
Now I am as you can see;
But please remember *all* of me.

Oliver Fairbrother

Oliver Fairbrother born in a bungalow
set in an avenue leafy with trees.
Father worked somewhere out in the city.
Mother taught Spanish and had three degrees.

Uncle brought books whenever he visited,
Aunt read him stories when he was just three.
He sat with the grown-ups and played silly games with them,
And had his own napkin when he sat down to tea.

He learned how to play on a rather large cello.
His parents applauded his performance in school.
He joined in with football, gymnastics and hockey
and learned how to dive in the town swimming pool.

They found him a place at the local academy,
Told him to work hard and always be good,
To do all the things that his teachers presented,
And learn all the things that a clever boy should.

He passed his exams with the help of his parents;
Got into Oxford and got a degree,
Then went into politics, encouraged by Father
and soon was selected for a constituency.

When he had his own children, he did just the same
as his parents had done to help him progress.
He read to them, played with them and joined in their dreams.
He knew that encouragement leads to success.

*

Oliver Fairbrother born in a bungalow
set in an avenue leafy with trees.
Father worked somewhere out in the city
Mother taught Spanish and had three degrees

Uncle brought sweets whenever he visited,
Aunt played pop music when he was just three,
He watched as the grown-ups played their silly games,
And went to bed sometimes without any tea.

He learned how to mess around in the classroom;
His parents got cross with his teachers in school;
He joined in with lads who played round in the churchyard
and learned that his friends liked him acting the fool.

They found him a place at the local academy
Told him that learning was simply for mugs;
To put up with school till he gets him a job.
The teachers are fools and the children all thugs.

He took few exams: none were helped by his parents.
He got him a job in a small local shop.
He bought cigarettes and beer with his pay packet
and drank all he could till he just couldn't stop.

When he had his own children he did just the same
as his parents had done for him, he couldn't do less.
They didn't want books, or sports kit or cellos
he just let them loose to continue the mess.

*

And so you can see the tiny percentage
That go on to fortune, fame and success,
Has little to do with a child's education:
It's what goes on outside that creates all the stress.
I know that it really is not very politic,
But you see it quite starkly wherever you roam.
Success in our schools or just abject failure
Is less in the classroom and more in the home.

We Made Forever

Antony, Graham, Westley and I
Went down to the wood on a sun-filled day.
We pitched our tent and lit a fire
To keep the worrying flies away.
We climbed some trees and we played our games
And lay in the sun till the sun went down.
We looked at the trees and gave them names,
And watched the moon rise over the town.
We had our supper and then we dreamed,
Floating away on a star-filled sky.
We made 'forever', or so it seemed,
Antony, Graham, Westley and I.

First Day

(Seven of us, all from the same class at school, met for coffee. Memories of those long, lost days formed this dedication to Ashmead School's class of 1956.)

First day; they all stand, shivering on the playground
in blazers far too large,
waiting for the teacher in charge to call.
The din from the shouting boys subsides
and all go in, to cower in the vastness of the hall.
It is a strange new world.

A class of boys, no noise; no one dares.
The slipper hanging on the blackboard shares its message with them all.
The first call of the new register throws out the names,
all new, unheard before. It stamps itself upon the memory for ever more,
and like an epic poem, burns itself upon the mind.
Each day, this ritual returns.

The corridor to the gym intimidates
with swirling frescoes of naked sportsmen clinging to the walls.
Calls from the showers echo from the hollow changing room.
Doom-laden vaulting horses, cliffs of wall-bars soaring to the ceiling,
further depress the inadequate feeling.

Like nightmare's dreams, erratic new experiences writhe and coalesce:
Quadratic equations rub shoulders with Pythagoras, white on black.
Beeswax and Bunsen burners, hoof-glue, sticky and grey, make the eyes run;
tins of powder paint and multi-coloured dyes
and the fun of art, or the art of fun;
the sinking mud of cross-country,
and the manic thrust of the scrum.
Touch the handle of the music room. Handel?
And 'Did you not hear My Lady go down the garden singing?',
with the metronomic beat of a drum.

Coffee around a table, and the recollections,
like the brown liquid, steam and flow.
That was all so long ago.
Mind-forming memories unite us all forever.
No experiences of the adult world can sever them.
No joy or horror can take those times away.
How grateful we are to have stood on the playground, on that first day.

The Pudding Club

Glistening cubes of ginger glory
nestle in waves of tangy cream,
generously infused with Cointreau.
Explore with your tongue, close your eyes and dream
your way through this heavenly syllabub.
Behind the glass the golden ginger beckons.
Feast with your eyes and ask for seconds.

Treacle slides slowly down golden sponge
from a dark, sweet-bubbled crater-crown on top.
Yellow custard, slightly steaming, streams from the jug
to wash a moonlit sea around this gin-soaked mound
that rises volcano-like from the plate.
Take a spoonful. Too late! You lose! The temptress wins
and smooth, sweet mouthfuls slide down in warm perfection.
Time to move on to the next confection.

Little white joys of softest apple
peep wistfully through golden, oaten crust,
lustfully bathed in pale rum sauce,
tantalizingly lurking in a dish.
Thrust in the spoon and make a wish.
Swoon on the heady fumes of alcohol, your inhibitions gone.
Just give your eyes a rub, and carry on.

Translucent crimson glory rises
phoenix-like from sherry-soaked sponge.
A tempting pink blancmange adorns this feat.
Lunge with the spoon and let the cold tang treat your tongue.
The night is young. No good heading for the door.
You're in the pudding club.

There's more and more and more!

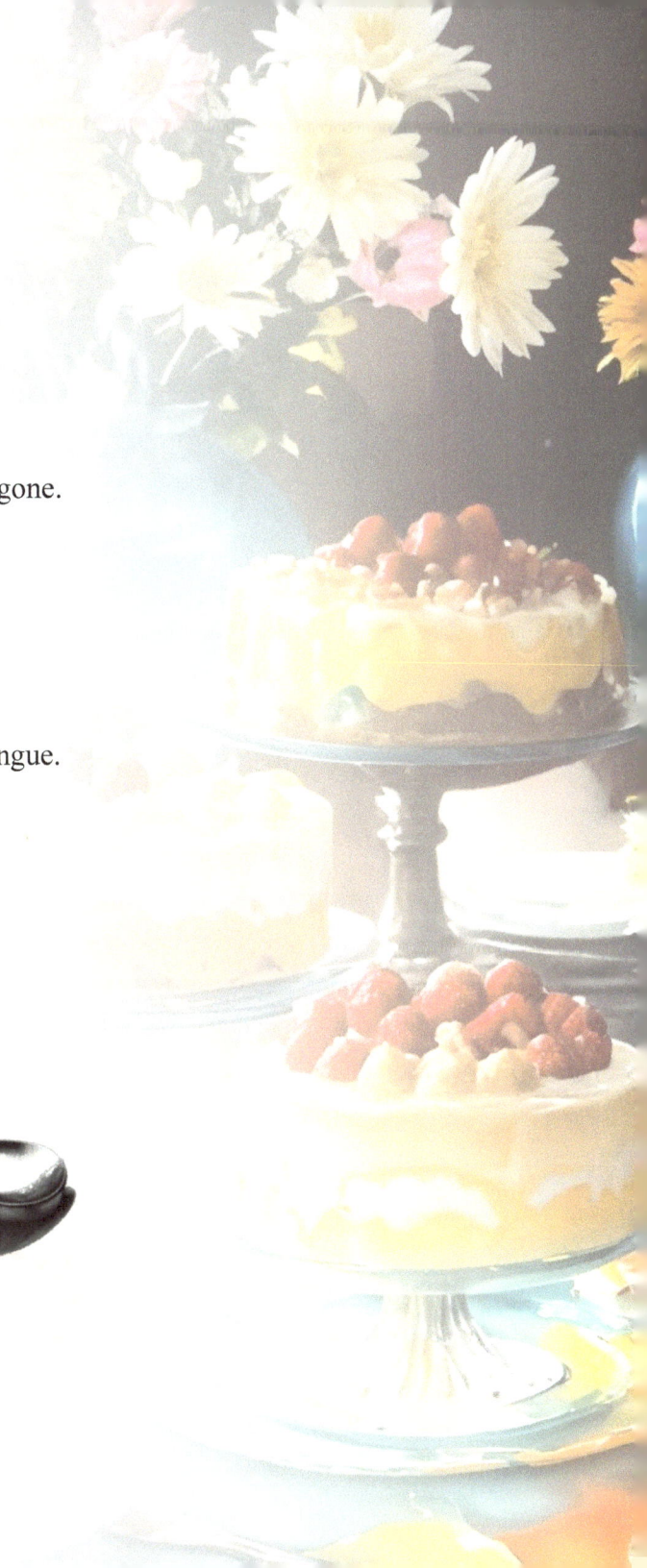

Also by Paul Wootten

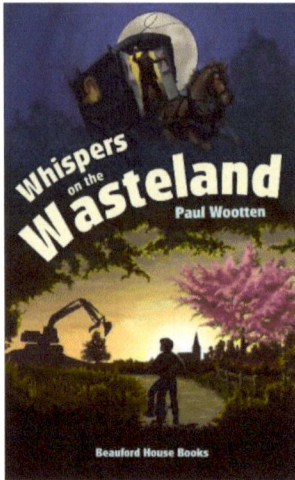

Whispers on the Wasteland

Tim has spent the last few years of his life travelling from place to place, following his father's job. He rarely stays long enough to make any friends, and now he's come to Wattleford where a patch of wasteland is marked for development. A natural playground for the children, it has, over the centuries, sheltered humans and wildlife amongst its trees and shrubs. Tim finds himself strangely in tune with the peoples of the past, but the town council has plans to develop the wasteland. Modern machines bring destruction and change, and Tim and his father are all that stand in their way.

Rogues on the River

David is terrified of the tramp under the bridge, and as a result of this, his adventures begin. He is forced into a whole new world of life on the river where he makes new friends, and battles with villainous rogues in post-war London. Following the end of the second World War, the towns are being rebuilt; bombed buildings hide behind battered sheets of corrugated iron, and the men have returned from the battle-fields. There is a feeling of optimism everywhere. Life is valued and children are treasured. They are often pampered and constantly shielded from danger. But danger finds David, one snowy winter's day.

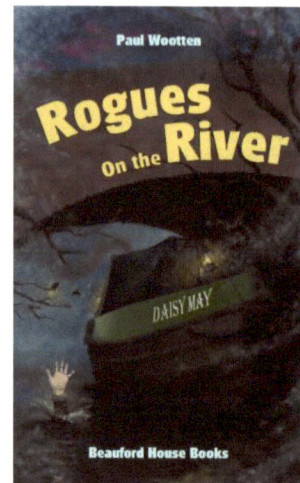

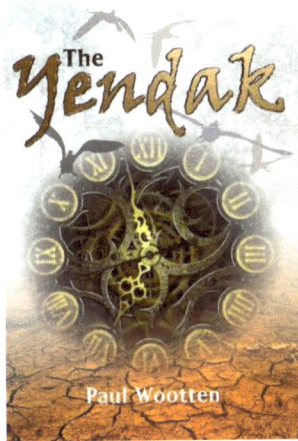

The Yendak

Christer has shared most of his young life with his cousin Sophie. But when his aunt remarries and they move away to a large house in the country, he feels a loneliness he has never known before.

Then Sophie becomes ill, slipping in and out of consciousness. Clutching at straws, his aunt hopes that the sound of Christer's voice might help to bring her round. He visits, as promised, and embarks on a quest for the mind of his cousin, lost somewhere in another dimension.

Following clues in her diary he plunges into a strange world of oppressed people, ruled by the Yendak, a cruel and violent race. If they find him, he will never get back home.

Acknowledgements

My thanks go to Antony for motivating and encouraging me to put these poems together. Without his hard work, this book would never have seen the light of day.

Antony's website: www.antonywootten.co.uk

www.ingramcontent.com/pod-product-compliance
Lightning Source LLC
Chambersburg PA
CBHW042022090426
42811CB00016B/1711

9 780993 504273